"I love to ride the ferry
where music is so merry.
There's a man who plays the concertina
on the moonlit upper deckerina."

— "Ferry Boat Serenade"

(words by Harold Adamson, music by E. DiLazzaro
© 1940 © renewed 1967 Robbins Music Corporation)

THE MOONLIT
UPPER DECKERINA

by

Naomi Lazard

The Sheep Meadow Press
New York City, 1977

ACKNOWLEDGMENTS:

These poems originally appeared in the following publications:

American Poetry Review: "The High Water Mark"
American Review: "At Your Party"
Big Moon: "Scenes from Life: III, IV, V"
The Chicago Tribune Magazine: "At Home"
The Hudson Review: "The Road," "The Pilot," "Letter/ March 1974"
The Iowa Review: "A Way of Life" (published under the title "The Way I Live Now")
Mademoiselle: "Stepping Out With My Big Cats," "Order in the Closet"
The Massachusetts Review: "Scenes from Life: I and II," and "The Covenant" (published under the title "The Last Covenant")
The Nation: "The Way I Am Lying Here," "The Wind," "Stray Dogs," "The Sisters" (published under the title "In the Waters of the Moon"), "The Embarkation" (published under the title "The Moonlit Upper Deckerina"), "The Terrible White Rose" (published under the title "The Flying Stars, the Terrible White Rose") and "A Stone for My Mother" (published under the title "My Face Breaks Apart")
The New Yorker: "The Arena," "The Angels Among Us," "Winter Visit With an Old Friend," "Walking With Lulu in the Wood," and "Looking for Itsy"
The North American Review: "Love Letter from the End of the World," and "Lines in the Edge of Winter" (published under the title "Lines in the Margin of Winter")
The Ohio Review: "Scenes from Life: VI"

"Letter/March 1974" was translated into Turkish by Talat Sait Halman. It was published in *Varlik* (Istanbul, Turkey)

Grateful acknowledgment is also made to the Creative Artists Public Service Program for their support.

for my dearest Amanda

Contents

I

II

Contents, *continued*

III

IV

I

"I once had a sparrow alight upon my shoulder for a moment while I was hoeing in a village garden, and I felt that I was more distinguished by that circumstance than I should have been by any epaulet I could have worn."
　　　　　　　　　　　　　　　　—Henry David Thoreau

The Angels Among Us

Outside the window the night burned
by lights, the ice trellis blooming,
white armature of dreams.
And there, moving darkly, one after one
over the horizon, the beautiful bands
lowering into distance.

The waves break over my head.
It is time to sail right out of the window
into the wake of the animals
who are leaving their paw prints to follow
in the snow. They are not far
from the north wind now,
keeping pace, nuzzling together.
The wind is the form of their speaking.

It is the night and the force
of these buildings that loosen
the tongue of the wind.
They are calling to me:
across marshland, savanna, tundra
and thicket, their language borne
on prayer and dust. I must answer
the beaver, who, hearing her babies crying,
gnaws her own flesh through to escape,
leaving a paw behind. The blood
on the trap is the edge of my dream.

Felines and rodents of woods and rivers
run across my body on whispering paws.
Even now they go quietly, disturbing no one.

As I fall in the slow revolution
of dreams, I am traced by a bullet,
I am cut by the hunter's knife.
I hear slaps of the trap. My cries
inhabit the rooms of sleep.

I struggle to wake with my eyes
against locked eyelids and madness.
They are calling to me, a sister,
come from the same endless labor
in the same primeval mud. I stand still
with my ears back, light and listening
with the wolves and the wolverines,
the minks, the otters, the beavers.
I spring on all fours. We are all
one now. In my dream I can dare
to lay my own throat bare to my enemy
as the wolves do.
                        It is too late.
I think of the lamb and of milk.
They are shaving the head of the lamb.
We are flying to the limits of night
from my own kind. Here, lungs on fire,
rung over rung inside the heart's glacier.
Here, where the dead bones glitter
in the magic center of the dream,
I see a sign. A flicker of stars,
pale and fluttering as a baby lamb.
I name them; the constellation
of animals—the angels among us.

Walking With Lulu in the Wood

The wood is a good place to find
the other road down to that hollow
which rocks a little with the same
motion as my soul. Come on, Lulu,
follow me and be careful of the rain
washed leaves. But you were always gentle.
I'll be quiet too and we won't disturb
the raccoons or any of the other animals.
I want to talk with the god here, Lulu.
This is a grove where he must be hiding,
and here is a pool for a small water god
to swim in. Let's talk with the god, Lulu.

The sun makes a great splash and you
are the one who is hiding in the tall grass
just the way you used to. Lulu,
you are the color of sand in a certain light,
like the shadow of light. The sun
is embracing me; the shadow also
means death. It is the god's word
in the language he speaks. He says
you are small again, that you have chosen it.
He says your reflection will be in the pool
forever, a blue resemblance, a startled joy.
He says this is your world now, this night
of tall trees, this cave of silences.
He says he loves you too; he watches you sleep.

Is the grove real? Is this your heaven, Lulu,
that you have let me enter? This glade,
the winter ivories? — the season you missed

by dying in the fall. Are these your jewelled
stones, your curled up animals, your grass?
And your god, the secret splash in the water
you always seemed to be listening for?
Is it the god's way—the mouth in the wood,
the opening to paradise?

God of animals and children, separations, loss.
Goodbye. Goodbye, sweet girl, again.
The days pass like oranges tossed
from hand to hand. Then one will drop
and it will be my turn. Wait for me here.
I hope to be fortunate, to come back and share
this winter wood with you, the dark hollow,
the snow dusted face of the god.

Stray Dogs

At three o'clock the field is white,
a front tooth spit out by the moon.
Where the grass will grow —
the rest is a blur of dark wool.
My eyes are held open by wires, my body
is stiff on the unyielding sheet.

In a matter of years it will be morning.

The dog sleeps, is sleeping
near the sea. Ringed with rocks
and the voices of fish, the dog sleeps
alone in the luminous night.

The dog dreams before dying, before
falling down to the fish, of a woman
in a blue bikini and a man
with a couple of humorous chins.
You, lumpy and hot beside me,
stoic and hot; at my feet in a mingling
of breath and flesh, the dog
roped round the neck, licking the salt
from my legs. We all sailed together
in a boat chug-chugging toward light,
to a mythical island, white as foam.
I cried, "They are going to abandon him!"

Somewhere in the future, in the morning,
your words repeat themselves,
"We can't stop for an unknown dog."

My bed sails across the Aegean
to the holy islands again. White houses
signal from the beach, white sheets
are shining in a windless sky.
I have watched the sheep with their heads up
and their mouths open. The bleached grass
is frightening. I've seen the dog
sprawled out in the shade of a rock.
I gave him my lunch but he was too unhappy
to eat. He never opened his eyes.

My bed moves in the storm of the sea,
the shore recedes between the waves.
We are still sailing together
in our uncertain boat that toils
back and forth among the islands.
Now and then we catch sight
of a house with a little steel trinket
above, that hopes to turn in the right wind.

The starving dog is our witness.
The crust of water is breaking.
We are falling, through waves,
down a thicket of fishes,
into the swollen dark.

Stepping Out With My Big Cats

And now in the dark shell of night,
in secret, I cast off from the shore
of my life. It is cool in this dark.
They are near me, my big cats, taller
than I am, my cougar, my leopards
and their cubs. They have come
to take me away down the branches
and plains of their memory. I walk
with them in step with their eyes
and their purring. Tonight
by a trumpet of moons we are bright
as chains linked together, moving
softly in and out of the mist.
I am quiet as moss, safe in the nest
of our walk. My big cats rub
the trees as we pass. They show
their teeth and I smile back.

Nothing and no one I have known,
no mystery of breath or glance,
leads me to this peace. Here
in the grace of an hour with them
I can enter my life's resting place.
My big cats give it all back to me
again, the brilliant mane of the wind,
the silence broken by sighs of the dew
spotted leaves. I touch their fur,
I see the world with their startled
and watchful eyes. This is the world
I want. This is the end of the dock
where I jump off out of my life.

Looking for Itsy

2 AM: the hour of rats
racing across alleys, junk
heaving in its graveyard, the hour
of strained bones like nerves whining
inside their shells of flesh.
2 AM: the dark hides nothing
but a lost cat, nothing but her whimper
as she runs to hide from the scarecrow buildings,
the rotten windows and the automobile parts
thrown into the block wide lot.

Into this desert we come, breathing hard,
the search party fanning out through the weeds
and the broken glass, calling one at a time —
"Itsy! Itsy! Itsy!"

There is no time for panic, we are fearless.
We must find her, she is lost and alone
in this metal jungle, the backyard of nowhere.
We are three shadows bent over
to see what the ashcans hide, pale under our hearts,
listening between heartbeats.

We step into a darker nightmare
as if from one hell down to another;
a dead cat screaming silently lying at our feet.
What's left is grey and white,
grey and white become the colors of our dread.
A dead cat frozen in the moonlight.

The moonlight
has become an enemy.
She is somewhere
hiding from the moonlight,
running from the moon
and the moon pursuing
like a thin white stranger
with a large hand sweeping
the shadows away.

She is somewhere
in this hell of rubble
where rats are boatmen
beating on metal rivers.
She is somewhere, breathing,
among this spiky junk,
an animal at bay
in a final thicket
where no leaves fall.

All night long we call her
up and down the alleys,
scared of the slithering rats
and the black doorways.
With hope gone like a candle
at the end of night
we call her and call her—
"Itsy! Itsy! Itsy!"

and take a vow in the milky light
of clouds turning pink with sunrise
to help every creature lost on the highways,
in the darkest sides of the city,
wherever there is no quarter.
We take the vow of helpfulness
and ask nothing in return,
not even the gift of Itsy found again.

Then like an answer we hear her calling
and see her perched on a pile of junk,
crying her dismay, so far from her own tree,
her kittens and her tuna fish.
We take her up and carry her off
into the morning, grown soft, and home.

The Way I Am Lying Here

I feel a dream coming into my bones
from long ago, before they were covered
with flesh, when they were small
as toothpicks, crossed over each other
in some kind of form without a name.

This dream emerging has a head
made of bone, soft in the center,
an opening with two sides
which must meet or clasp
in something like friendship.
I see the cleft no bigger than a hair
and the two sides straining together.

These little bones move
with delicate steps; now
it is too late to retrieve
a husk or a shell, to crawl
away from the backbone, leave
this armature lying
flat on the bed with one leg
drawn up like a stork.

It is too late and yet
I have this yearning
for an earlier form, two
breathing valves, the crisp
body made of joints, no flesh
to spoil. Not a bird, not
any kind of a beast, nor a fish.

These are the forms close enough
to my own; I know how they betray
in the end, how what's underneath
is left speaking of sadness.

In my dream I was sure
as the moon which is no more
than a dimple of light, as sure
as the walls which expand and contract
to the whim of the clouds.
There is the truth of the skull,
the tibula, the rib-cage and the thorn
on the leg called an ankle.

It is the truth that knots
in my heart when I see the crumpled
remains of a rabbit or the lean,
fleet skeleton of a horse or a deer.
It is the knowledge locked
in the marrow, that moves
with my foot, rises on both legs
while my body, half a ghost already,
is going into the air.

The Covenant

for the wolves

The sun marks the sea with a sign,
last bright sickle of light.
We go quickly across the domain
of waters, the wind a stick
in my hand, fast as your fur

and my hair can fly. What a bird
would say I feel on my lips;
the words breaking out in pairs,
two by two as those other animals
went from the flood. Moonlight

flickers and melts on the air;
one final leap into the deep night
and we hit land. Now we're creeping
like sap from a tree while the ground
is wet underfoot, and the beetle's

sound is a gong. On our knees
in the end, back to the roots
of the heart. This is the place,
the wind made flesh, the greens
and all movement are one.

We can just see the brilliant
faces of cubs looking out.
All night I must kneel at the gates
of the house without doors. Morning
comes like a knife between my eyes.

13

I must roll back my tongue
and forget my own language of lies.
Then my body remembers, my feet
grow as sure as your own of these
deepest retreats where we all sleep

together. The ways of the trees
open for me, defying the guns,
the numbers of enemies
who are stalking the woods
where we live now as we should live,

our bodies close as the ringing
of bells. I am one with you
at last, a guardian of paradise,
with a helmet of fiery leaves
and nothing more. I know

we will not survive. I see us
already ablaze, trapped
in a circling fire. The killers
stand on its edge, fixing the sights.
We are caught where the black lines

cross. We have only this moment.
You push your face into my hand.
I hold you hard at my side,
kiss you, bless you again.
A cry holds us both in its arms.

II

A Stone for My Mother

The frozen lake and the sky
cracked by the grey wind.
My face breaks apart too
in the mirror and you are there
again, winter after winter,
your bones behind my skin.

The steel clouds freeze
like your memory in me,
the sallow flesh indentured.
It was life's signature
of suffering on you, the wounds
you scratched, that bled

but never healed. As your wrists
inside my own scratch me.
What matters is this skeleton
of night, my pillow bent
to hold you down so you can't fly
away. The night cannot contain

your cries. Only my body can hold
you down, my fractured face
so weak already from your bones
crumbling. You are waiting
to be released, to be born
out of my body. I rush outside

to find the right place
to let you out. I see you
as you were in cheap cafeterias,
the woman in front of me without
a coat. Or that one huddled
under a leaky umbrella. I see you

poor as always, curved and hopeless,
weeping without a sound. It is
your heart, twin to my heart.
We are walking past windows
that flash the dark back on your glasses
I broke once with a stone.

The Embarkation

The rustle of doves ascending,
a light breaks out in my brain.
Gently, like blood, a hammer
beats there. Arms divide into wings
and lift me beyond the weight
of my body. All around is the swell
of other departures, the quickening

crowd on its way to the pier.
Grandfather, dressed all in white
to match his beard, checks us in
with his blessing and his faith
in a fine passage on a prosperous
sea. On this shore two frogs sing.
Yesterday there was no sound

but lamentation. It was our lives,
broken on wheels. But tonight
is the night of the lamb, of tired
horses, the night of the poor,
the moment between the last star
and the sun when the bread and the staff,
the flower and the peach,

the farewell and the promise
become one. All my life the days
crept by on hands and knees
in a kind of madness; I stood
holding their shells to my ear.
A faint roar remained like the echo
I was waiting to hear. Darling,

at last we are together at this rail,
the sea tilting smoothly away,
the waves advancing. At our side
the silky bodies play again, the animals
we love. We are here to sail
the crystal ship to the land of lands.
Glass sails unfold like light,

banners tinkling on the air.
We catch the wind in our hands
and toss it back to where it beats
upward forever, to the center
of the mind's eye, to the tiny
ship reflected there and all of us
together, joined in the dance.

Grandfather thumps out the pace
on his good leg. Crickets are busy
and nestlings chirp to keep the time.
From the prow a lantern swings
like a single flame. Good sailors
already, we roll with the swaying
slippery deck of the ark.

Lines in the Edge of Winter

for Eugene

It's the end of autumn now,
the wind breaks free. Treetops
scribble wildly on the line of sky.
Silently the bears are coming
along the footpath, searching

for winter. Is this my shadow
sticking to the ground, my arms
hanging loose, my own head splintered
by light? Is it me at last listening
for the bears? I want to go with them

as they do their slow step
of accepting. Last year I thought
I could walk on water, my life
a pastel tinted photograph I carried
in front of me. That didn't last.

I am still the same, waiting
between the sheets for your letter,
sleeping in a strange bed that feels
like the floor. When morning raps
my window and calls me back to order

I'll creep outside again, lost
after that rough trip by moonlight.
Nothing went right. I screamed
at the devil who was only doing his job,
offering me another life. He is clever

but this is the life I want.
I want to be with the bears,
this winter. If you have no time
for a letter, send me the envelope
with your name on the back.

It will tell me that I must be here,
that the bears are preparing,
that you too will move into the first
snow fall, your head of a Persian king
lowered and your black marble hair

curling. Dear friend, your steps
will fall away from you into winter
where the bears will find them.
They need them as I do
for the white and mystic dance.

The Sisters

She will be a scholar, and I
a good for nothing like my father.
She is gifted with lemon hair
and cleverness. I must learn
not to expect too much.

She will be enough for them,
the one like a yellow lily.
They bend their necks and say
snow will turn into doves for her.

                              Meanwhile
there is time for us to sit and listen
to the hours as they pipe the green months,
time to feel the spring reaching us
and beyond us, blowing dandelions.
We play a game under the dining room table
in the room behind the candy store.
We are deep in our waterfall.
The silvery fish jump and surface,
plunge to feed on the anemones.
The skirt of the rock facing our face,
brocaded with violets, hides us from sight.
We know the living stream.
We build a city every day
on the edge of that waterfall.

We are two queens.
We have a secret niche
above a secret barrel.
We keep our crowns there.

When the afternoon blows like dust outside,
when the sleeping windows close,
one queen walks her china doll,
step by step, to the executioner.
The dark queen commands;
the gilded one must lose her head again.

Sister like a water lily,
how clever life is at last.
On this winter day the four
uncurtained windows shine across
the miles between us. Four empty windows;
one has an avocado plant inside.
A shadow moves across the glass;
the woman is at home.

It is twilight where you are.
The sky falls in upon the tallest
buildings without a sound. Soon
looms of darkness spin
along the darkened ground.
Getting older should make more difference.

There is another daughter now,
your flickering girl of seven.
She has no sister, no china doll.
She has the name we dreamed about
as children, as if she had jumped
out of our waterfall
like one of those silvery fish.

A Way of Life

I know these shadows well,
the darkest corner is familiar
The bit of light through the blind,
the scent of pomander; this
is my bedroom. You are with me.

I am making a statue of you
out of your own body, commemorating
the precise feeling of the surface
of your skin, your head turning,
the shape of your thighs, your
back and shoulders. Your flesh
keeps dissolving under my hands;
it is striving toward memory,
toward completion which I cannot
reach. I keep forming you again,
out of your own substance, elusive
as the crucial fragment
in a half remembered dream.
The role you play in this process
is as active as mine, you
are straining upward with the effort
to experience your creation.
This is the way you will burst out
of yourself; you never do this.
It is my constant failure.

Your face is most difficult,
the head is extremely hard to get.
Already your face is not the one
I remember. My own fingers confuse me

as I trace the curve of your forehead.
Your eyes confound me. They fly away
as I touch them.

          My bed is breaking
with the weight of this problem.
I am lying on splinters.
I want you to know that all this
means something. It is my life's work.

The Room

With my shadow hand I draw the room
as it is; wall hung with prints,
two windows side by side, blinds
down and dark. This is where we are
together, the room of the dream
where in the morning
I'll wake with a light heart.

Here is the other room, beginning
to come true; down the stone stairs
worn in the center. Here it is all
stone, stone beds, slabs for tables,
lower chunks for chairs.
Everything is small as childhood toys,
cozy as a doll's house. Here
is where we can eat, sleep, cook
with the alabaster dishes
and the marble tea cups.

Strangers will crack open the seal,
knock down the heavy door,
creep into our darkness, find us
stretched out soft as children
on the stone bed.

The High Water Mark

It isn't so much that I think about you
all the time, that I miss you,
long for you, for your hands,
your face coming down at me,
body closing in with all its light.
It isn't so much that I love you,
that I carry you around
like a seventh sense, which
though I try to contain it
runs ahead, a spinnaker shuddering
with its own life, mad in the wind
with something like joy.

It isn't that I adore you
so much or that you are my darling,
my passion, as that I swim into you
like a new born fish
just hatched out of the pearly pile.
　　　You couldn't have known
when you saw me first, lying
flipped on one side, only one round eye
visible, mouth hanging open, drowning
slowly in all this blackness.

Look, I've had to learn an entire repertoire
of ways to be, to take grace
from your hand when it comes to catch me
with its little hook, when it shakes off
my new dress of sequins,
when it slides like a waterfall,
loosens the seaweed from the moon on the water,

when the strands hold and tangle
for sea miles everywhere
and the dark pitched bells and spouting whales
turn frantic in the somber ocean,
I must not expire
but breathe in and out just like before.

Love Letter from the End of the World

I want you to understand
how it's been with me, how I came
to a place I knew was going to kill me.
I stayed as long as I could.
It was the starving cats that kept
me there, the donkeys crying,
the roosters who didn't know
day from night anymore.

That island was highly recommended
for its dazzling rocks. The sea
kept me alive, some wise clams,
fierce little sea urchins that stuck
their spines into me. The tiny hands
of the sea kept my body alive all night
while I listened to the donkeys weeping.

The genius of the sea
slipped into my brain, loved it
with sea kisses. It wasn't too late.
I invented you; a sudden inspiration
needing only a quick jab on my life
to get it going. You shot out
of the empty spaces between
the valves of my heart.

I keep on inventing you,
describing you over and over to myself.
You keep me alive now. I know how
you wake up in the morning.

your long back flicking from one side
to another, opening your eyes all at once
like a child, because it's a new day

and it is enough. I write you
love letters which you never answer.
No sign, no envelope with your name on it.
No falling stars, no comet,
nothing predicted at all this year.
When you turn out your lights
the walls, papered with my love letters,
will glow after you in the dark

because I am still inventing you,
describing your voice for myself,
writing scripts for it that have no end.
Here it is the end of the world.
The donkeys are crying, the cats
in Hydra are still starving. You
are near your window looking down

at the street, holding my most recent
love letter. I say, "My darling,
Allende is dead. Pablo Neruda too,
the journal of his days destroyed.
Nobody you know is in the street.
It is our Saint Bartholomew's night
of the soul. My country is suffering
from leprosy. We all carry bells."

III

Scenes from Life

I

We are living in a furnished room
under assumed names. We have a dirty
window and a brick wall facing it.
It is always dusk here. I have come
to be with you to get away from myself.
I am fascinated by your loneliness.
The brick wall is marching
toward us. I cook supper on the hot plate.
I cry at night. I have an abortion.

You have the idea that when you get rich
our lives will change. Nothing
can stop you.
                    My train leaves at seven o'clock.
You take me to the station. We stand
surrounded by steam rising. I am falling
onto the track. You hold my hand lightly.

The train is taking me away from you;
it is taking me into the snow, across
trees and frozen lakes. The track
bends with the horizon.

I return and you are rich, with a wife
and two children. You are disconsolate.
You send them away for a vacation
so we can get to know each other again.
We get to know each other again.
We have a furnished room over the river.

You let the river run through my hair.
The sun turns you into gold.
What a dilemma.

You are a good boy. You have taken
your vows. I am an intruder
in your temple. It is so quiet here.
I can't keep quiet enough. Your gods
call me a bad girl because I left you.
They have forgotten how lightly
you held my hand. They have forgotten
the abortion.
     Your gods are stronger
than you are; their enormous shadows
fill this place. Your loneliness
becomes a gospel. You sleep with it.
You take it between your teeth
like a treat.

II

I am still half asleep, my body
is not a part of me. It is rising
alone. I unwind all my hair and listen,
something shivers inside my robe.
My head is on the window with its eyes out.
You are the stranger at my door.

You enter my kitchen, holding
the moon in your hands. I crouch
near the stove, stirring my usual
midnight meal. We are melting
together in the pot—me in my yellow
bikini, you with your restless glance—
two thickening specks in the soup.

This is my home now, my work,
my booming sky out there beyond
the lights that flicker in the night.
There is no end to that dark;

                                we are flying in it,
flying so slowly, the desperate
profile of one cloud turns
with my own movement.

                              Look,
you can see the wavering wood as well,
where it leans down to the autumn deer.
We are there; we crept on our knees to hide,
transparent over the cliff side.
Soon it will be dawn,
the banners will furl
on the dancing land.

My closets are full of sleep, my dreams
loaded with ships, with sails.
My bed is filled with your hands.
The kettle is boiling. Let's drink
up the sea while it's still hot.
My love, let's kiss the flesh
of these ghosts. Let's eat.

III

I am lying stretched out on the floor
when you enter. I step into the fire
to greet you. The fire is not
in the fireplace; it is in my body.
The brown wood of the floor turns red,
the line along your cheekbone is orange.
Your hair is darkening. Your eyes
belong to your mother;
they were left behind when she was put
into her grave. They are telling me
that we have grown old, that we have
no wisdom. You close your hand
over the flesh of my arm.
Your back is curved as you sit
facing me; the curve says
you are the keeper of my death.

You are watching me get sick and die
of cancer; you watch my teeth fall out.
You are my mirror where I see
my face failing.

                  An ember is shaking
itself loose from my throat. Further down,
inside my lungs, the fire burns faster.
The ember lodges in my throat
like a lozenge. I am waiting for it
to dissolve, to spit it up, to light
the fire from my mouth to yours.

Your eyes are becoming red.
I see that the outsides of your eyes
have died already. What is alive
is the center, that shifts like water.
It is the changeless, liquid blue.

The cry that climbs and falls in you
embraces me with broken words.
I believe them though my questions
are never answered. You take the fresh
fire of my body and loosen it
from its bones. I hang from your arms.
I believe in the fire. I believe
in your red eyes, in your thick and flecked,
your goldhaired butcher's hands.

IV

The wind is obscene today. It is
looking for you everywhere,
screaming into the rocks and over
the mountains, howling your name.
I am sprawled out under the sun
listening to the wind searching for you.
The wind thinks I can't hear
but I have nothing to listen to
except those tearing cries.
I am lying on my back, my body
oiled and shining, waiting for your answer.

I am defeated by the wind.
I telephone you. "I think I will die
today," I tell you. "I called to say
goodbye forever." Your laugh resembles
the static on the line, you are far away.
Your voice is leaving you; it carries
your hat in its hands, a polite gesture.
"Don't say things like that," you say.
"Have a good time."

I lie down with the sun again.
The sun presses me flatter. I hear
the telephone ringing in your room again.
You answer. It is the wind speaking
on the wires. My life stretches
out under the sun, over the wires
connecting the distance that unites us.
The sun soaks up my mind like a blotter.
The ink is not quite dry. I know
what is written there so well; I can
read it backwards and forwards
and upside down.

V

There are twin beds but we only use
one of them. We have taken this room
for a few hours; finally you must go home.
''You are the only person who makes me
happy,'' you say when we leave. We go out
into the night like trapeze artists
with no fear of falling.

I am going away for two weeks
so you can straighten out your life.
You take the news well, you are cheerful.
You keep your appointment
with your therapist; you take
your older child to the theatre.
Your life appears to hold its breath;
the heaving has stopped.
You come home on time every night.
Your wife stops poisoning your food.

You eat hearty lunches with the boys
at the office. Your footsteps crunch
the thick snow. My climate is different.
I am dyeing my skin Mexican brown.
Stones keep me company.
I live inside of them; sometimes
their silence enters me as if I were a cave.
I fall asleep with your leg crossed
over my own. You turn your back
to your wife and change the channel.
Sometimes you notice I am not there.

VI

I have discovered a lump on my breast
about the size of a cocktail onion.
I am always aware of it.
I can feel it with the flesh
on the inside of my upper arm.
My heart beats inside of it.
And I thought I might live to be
fifty or sixty. I took a lot
for granted, the two of us for example,
strolling together in some late afternoon.
I assumed we would be living
in a Mediterranean city near a beach.

Now I have this lump. I remember
my mother sitting at the kitchen table
with her head bent into her arms.
Her arms cross each other; her head
is very heavy. Now I understand
what she meant by sitting like that.

My lump is very heavy for its size.
I see those swallows again forming
statues in the air and then dispersing
to sing against the solitude of separations.
I think about sand crumbling
inside my fingers. I can taste it
brushing my hand across my face.

There is always the sun, a late sun
when it looks like a discus
tossed by some enormous player
over the water. Kites are flaring
in the distance; runners gasp at the strings.
My darling, we were to have been fortunate
and hear their cries.

In my dream I was lying lightly
in the middle of the sounds of crickets;
medals of moonlight slipped along
my thighs. The moorings of the sailing boats
rock against the harbor, lights
of many mornings break against the shutters.
Summers are going by, lazy white dirigibles
floating past us.

                                  The gulls

are still sweeping red hoops
low on the horizon, while now
the sun whirling right over my head
makes red hoops inside my eyes.

IV

*"To say what you want to say you must create another
language and nourish it for years with what you have
loved, with what you have lost, with what you will never
find again."*

—George Seferis
Days: 1945-51

Missing Father Report

Your help is urgently needed.
If you have any information
regarding the whereabouts
of the following individual
contact us immediately.

Subject is, or was, about 45
at the time of disappearance.
Last seen dissolving slowly,
first the back of his neck;
then his shoulders went away,
his legs left too. In the end
his face vanished without warning,
the mouth open, still speaking.

We have no indication why
this person, of all people,
should have disappeared.
Reliable witnesses have stated
that not even his eyes endured,
not even the tips of his fingers.

You will know him by certain signs,
by the innocent look of his hair
falling over his forehead
in moments of emotional upheaval,
by his hands which are fine
and arrive like delicate instruments
of mercy.

You will also know him
by his eyes which have an unblinking
quality like those of a horse
or some other friendly, domesticated
animal. You will know him
if you are prepared.

There is no history of mental disease,
no police file. Disappearance was,
for all practical purposes,
voluntary. Subject's last
formal statement, for the record,
was "I love you,"
or something like that.

The Wind

When the wind howls at the window
with your mother's voice,
when she knocks there with her shoe —
don't leave her out in the cold.
Though you never said anything
she was glad to hear, though
you stopped trying to please her
before you started school, let her in.
It is your life she is battering
with her sad muddy shoe on the panes.
As if you truly need her, as if you mean it,
make room for her in the bed beside you.
She won't open her eyes.
When you take her in your arms
she will fall apart like ashes.
Best not to touch her;
make a hollow in your pillow
for her dust to settle in.
It will be just a spoonful,
enough to stir into your coffee
when you wake up in the morning.

Letter/March 1974

My dearest sister,
it is a cornflower afternoon;
the year has gone around again.
This is another anniversary
of singing fish and dreams of fireflies.

Friends are here to help me bear it.
How our lives stretch back of us,
banners like ships riding
on a sea of faces. Between the deaths
and all the other separations,

an orange light lifts me beyond
myself sometimes. Other times not.
Darling sister, what did you have in your mind
when you moved to that other country?
I had to carve out my own voyages,

and all the time I thought
we were to be together in the end.
The end is not so far away now;
it is beckoning to me, just around the corner.
I see our last house standing

where it should be, surrounded by forest,
filled with the sounds of our animals.
We must hurry or it will be too late
if we are to have any of it. Hurry,
dear sister, the cats are hungry.

the dogs need their exercise. The forest
animals are waiting for us, the foxes
are in danger. Young deer are being slaughtered
for lack of our presence. Why wait
until we are hags and can't run

with the little ones? It will be good
for the children, learning to nourish
the living. I say enough of this ruination;
No to this life that has no center.
Don't wait any longer. This

is the true wilderness, the world
turning dark. Send me your answer.

The Arena

You can't decide whether or not
to leave your wife. She is not beautiful
to you. She is boring; she has devoted
herself to the A and P, to Friday night
pizza. She is so boring, you think
she has gone crazy. You are not crazy.
You always knew you never loved her.

As soon as I saw that squalor
you live in I knew it wasn't
going to be possible for you
to pry yourself loose.
You have been studying the matter
however, giving it grave and serious study.
You are examining your life
from the point of view of several philosophies.

Now you have gone to the trouble
of hiring an arena, and have ordered costumes.
The staff of experts alone is costing you
a fortune. But this is the way you want it,
the whole works, a full orchestra
and original music for the occasion.
Everyone must be paid equity wages.
You've had the whole place draped
in bunting. I think the color you have chosen
is bad but I don't say anything.

I didn't realize you were so keen
on pomp. Your life is so perfectly ordinary,
cornflakes and sliced banana for breakfast,
then the commuter bus. To stimulate
your imagination, the New York Times
and the Wall Street Journal. I suppose
I should have known there was something
more dramatic behind your hooded eyes.

This is it then. It's to be the arena.
You will arrive alone, your robe
embroidered and flowing, in your sedan chair.
Your wife doesn't need to be pursuaded,
she feels this drama even more sharply
than you do. She can't wait for the spectacle
in the costumes you've chosen for us.
She wants to tear my eyes out.
She wants to shoot me
with the gun you have given her.

The great day is approaching.
Already your friends are hawking tickets
in the streets. I see there are posters
stuck up in windows of laundries
and drugstores. Such a bad job.
My name isn't even spelled right.

I've just heard something else.
You have ordered ten thousand oversize
thumbs which will be given out
to the spectators. And not only that;
you have bought five or six lions
and you are not feeding them.

My poor darling, they will turn on you.
You'll be reported to the humane society.
Besides, you will be paying for this
forever. They will garnishee
your income tax deductions.

All this is beside the point.
The point is I have never even met
your wife. And she is a woman like me
with her own sorrows.
I am handicapped already.

If I can somehow get to her
before the day of the arena
maybe we can work out something
together. No. It is hopeless. She knows
things will never be the same again.
Even the cornflakes will taste
of sawdust and disaster.

The Pilot

You say you are a pilot on a dangerous mission.
Night after night you've got to make the run
from one beleaguered city to another,
flying through enemy flak, the red and orange
bursts, the air shuddering and tilting.
Those experts manning the anti-aircraft
are incredible sharp-shooters.

Just a few nights ago your plane was hit.
Only your courage, your daring and expertise,
brought the old crate in.
And all the crew was safe.

I understand about your terrible work,
how much it takes out of you,
the nightmares that scream in your sleep.
I sympathize with your burden of responsibility
for the out-dated crate you must fly,
and the crew. I've even grown to admire
that despot, the sour-faced navigator
without whom, as you've told me
with characteristic modesty,
you might never make it.

I know you are a hero.
I know these flights are genuinely frightening.
I know they take your breath away
and make you speechless. I know
your silences are a burden to you;
sometimes you are suddenly stricken
by one of them. Then you sit there,

your mouth locked in the open position,
locked like your plane zooming down
with the throttle all the way forward
in order to ride with the plunge
through the sound barrier.

Because of all this I want to make it easy
for you. It isn't necessary to say anything.
If you love me, just tap one time
with a finger or a foot.

At Your Party

You invited me to your party
because you love me. You say
you love my arms, the lines
on my forehead, the joints
of my fingers. You say you could
recognize me anywhere by my slightest
sound or gesture. I believe you.
I feel the same way about you.
So I come to your party with gifts.
You are so happy I have come.
You take the flowers I have brought
and immediately press them
between two slabs of marble.
I make a note of this
but I don't want to be distracted.
I am all here, right now,
with you at your party.

Your party is a pretty informal
affair, and it goes on a long time.
At one point you lean over to me
and whisper, "This can't go on
much longer. We'll be alone soon."
And you pass me one of your hands
to hold for you, a sort of a hostage.
I slip it under my skirt
where it can warm me a little
and won't be too noticeable.

At last they are all gone.
You lift me off the ground
with your one remaining hand.
I return the one I've been holding
for you so you can lift me better.
This is the moment we've been waiting for.

You take me into the private wing
of your house. It is musty here, dark
and airless. You start turning
lights on and I see that this part
of your house looks like a warehouse
or a barracks. It is very somber.
"Do you think we can have any fun here?"
I ask. "Fun," you say. "Who said anything
about having fun."

We go further into this room and I see
that it is cavernous. There are dim
regions that defy being lighted.
My eyes grow accustomed
to the dark; in the shadows
there are photographs of me and of you.

In these photographs we look carefree,
innocent and very young. I don't remember
taking all those photographs.
"I have been true," you say, "to our youth.
You have been false." You are laughing
as you say this. I can't be sure
what you are doing when you say one thing
and act as if you have said another.

I try to get things straight.
"I thought you loved me," I say.
"It would be a great victory for me
if I could give you up," you answer.
Now I understand the distance
that divides us.
                        Now I notice
that along the walls you have accumulated
furniture. I see that it is furniture
from another time, old junk, rickety.

You begin to take yourself apart.
You give me one of your hands again,
first asking me which one I prefer.
You take your eyes out and put them
on a table. You take out your voice,
your entire rib cage including your heart,
and put them away in a drawer.
You stand in front of me with your chest
gaping. "Help me with my head," you say.
"It is so heavy. I want to take it off
so I can rest." I can't move.
The distance between us is growing greater.
You are struggling with your head,
trying to get it off. "I can't help you,"
I say. "If only you loved me enough,"
your voice says from the drawer.

Order in the Closet

It is half-past my lifetime,
dark, everyone is tucked in
for the night. I have said
whatever prayers I ever learned;
now I'll make some order
in the closet though I'm fed up
with everything there. My clothes
drip inanely from their hangers.
They weren't meant to be like this.
I had hopes once for a lovelier me,
for great scenes, reconciliations,
homecomings, splendid meetings,
lunches. The deft strokes
of fortune that startle
when least expected.

There is nothing left to do
except sift through these oddments
that have failed me.
This adventurous suit is the worst,
last season's madness —
when I wore it yesterday
it walked me into mirrors.
I saw the piled up bones
of my desire marching toward me.

So I strip the closet clean
and leave it gaping,
a dark hole in the wall
just long enough to lie down in.
I can sleep here
in the honest bareness of the place,
covered with my crazy quilt
of wire hangers, each one
a fishing hook. The big fish
still fly in the water.

At Home

I live on the 13th floor
in a building that has no 13th floor.
I have lived here all of my life.
I was born here in the space
between two regular floors.
The elevator doesn't stop here;
nobody knows there is a 13th floor.

You have to be very industrious
to live here. Walking up and down
all those flights of stairs isn't any joke.
I have strong legs but some of the others
in my family couldn't wait until they got out
even though it meant being carried out,
dead or screaming.
                    The trouble
with moving from the 13th floor
is that when you sign up for another place
you can't give a previous address.
Nobody believes you when you tell them
where you've been living.
They think you are nobody, that you
are lying, that you are some crazy
psychopath who may very well shoot them.

I had a husband too for a while
but the 13th floor wasn't for him.
He wanted the big time, the class
of an even number. I let him go.
He left with my only piece of luggage,
our monogrammed sheets and towels.

I'll never make it out of here.
I've made my home as cozy as possible.
It is filled with chintz framed photographs,
lace bedspreads for dreaming, filigree
curtains and other kitsch.
I've developed a real style here,
an emulation of normalcy.

I am not one of your neediest cases.
Don't send care parcels or helpful hints
about positive thinking. I have my work,
my plans. I am sending out flyers
for an event that will take place soon.
Everyone is invited. No RSVP necessary.
Just come as you really are.

The Road

It's been a long time since we missed
the turning. The road is dividing
everywhere, the hills are becoming
bleaker. The back of your head is tense
with watching for the signs, your hands
on the wheel are tight. You have lost
your humor. I won't say, "I told you
this would happen." I won't say,
"Let me take over." I am not encouraged
by your profile. If I had a song
left in me I would sing it.
But you don't want a song. I can tell
by your eyelids that you are disgusted.

I am following you in another car.
It is the worst time for driving, just
between twilight and night. Everything
I've learned is no use to me.
Your car is eating up the road
and spitting it back to me.
Small animals keep darting out
from the bushes, my headlights
are reflected in their terrified
eyes. "Go back!" I scream.
"This is no place for you!"

The night is furious with us
and sends down rain to make us feel
like beggars. We are sitting in a diner
having a cup of coffee.

"Where
are we going?" you ask. I was about
to answer, "We are going to Ithaca," or
"I thought you knew," but I think
better of it. Instead I say,
"We are going to your mother's grave.
We will grieve for all of us.
Everything will be all right."

Winter Visit With an Old Friend

Home is the two horned moon
drifting down the horizon—
that slip of a boat resembling
sleep. You must be near me now,
rushing across the bare treetops.
It is the darkest part of the night,
the moment I expect you to appear.

You king of the odd hour,
where are you with your hundred
years of the saddest news?

I wake with a gasp.
Here you are, pushing my dreams
out of your way, with the flower
of your own frost in your hands
like the offering of a chalice.
You bring me this.

So much bad news!
Why should I need you too?

Later tonight I'll be working,
performing open-heart surgery
on myself—first the slit
in the flesh, exposing membrane
and muscle, then to take
the throbbing thing itself
apart with all the blood there,
and make the final incision.

Down with all that.
The purple and gold
happiness wasn't true.

The Terrible White Rose

I was a knot on an endless string;
you were a cloud without any edges.
My life had frozen in place,
the wind stiff on my pillow.
Let's sleep here, you said,
with the flying stars, the terrible white rose.

I was home in the ordinary way
from a poisonous trip, simple at last,
free for your restless hair. Our shadows
slid on the grass; we carried the rain
in our hands, kept a watch on the temple
of birds that gleamed in the sky.

Let's move in, you said, so we did.
We crept to a hill to hide, lay
in our borrowed hole for a while.
Oh, for a ship, for a sail, for a hand!
For a voice, for a touch, for you,
for the flying stars, the terrible white rose.